CONTENTS

4

I WANT TO KNOW...

?

What was it like before cars?

Paul Humphrey
and
Alex Ramsay

First published in this edition in 2011 by
Evans Publishing Group
2A Portman Mansions
Chiltern Street
London W1U 6NR

© Evans Brothers Limited 2011

www.evansbooks.co.uk

British Library Cataloguing in Publication Data
A CIP catalogue record for this book is available from the British Library

ISBN: 9780237544904

Planned and produced by Discovery Books
Cover designed by Rebecca Fox

For permission to reproduce copyright material the author
and publishers gratefully acknowledge the following: Beamish, The North of England Open Air
Museum: pages 11, 13, 17, 18, 27; istock: cover; Mary Evans Photo Library: pages 7, 9, 23; London
Transport Museum: page 17; Peter Newark's Historical Pictures: page 25; Topham Picture
Source: page 21

Printed by Great Wall Printing Company in Chai Wan, Hong Kong,

August 2011, Job Number 1672.

It won't take us long in the car. Everybody travels so fast nowadays. When my grandpa was your age a journey to the seaside could take all day.

Were there cars then, Grandpa?

Yes, but not many people had them. The cars went very slowly. To start the engine you had to turn a handle at the front.

The cars didn't have roofs, so when it rained you had to put the hood up.

Most roads weren't covered with smooth black tar like they are now.

They were very bumpy and in summer they were very dusty, too.

Yes, they did! They had to wear goggles to keep the dust out of their eyes.

In those days most shops
would deliver the shopping.
People ordered what they
wanted and a boy from the
shop would ride over on a
bicycle with the shopping.

Yes, he did, but it was very different from yours. The bikes in those days didn't have any gears and some didn't even have brakes!

12

13

Cycling was uncomfortable then. The streets were made of cobblestones and they were very bumpy. Cyclists had to be very careful not to get their wheels caught in the tramlines, too.

Tramlines were like railway lines except that they were laid in the road. Trams would run along them.

What is a tram?

A tram was like a bus, but it ran along tramlines. The driver rang a bell to tell you to get out of the way.

Before cars, people often travelled by tram or bus.

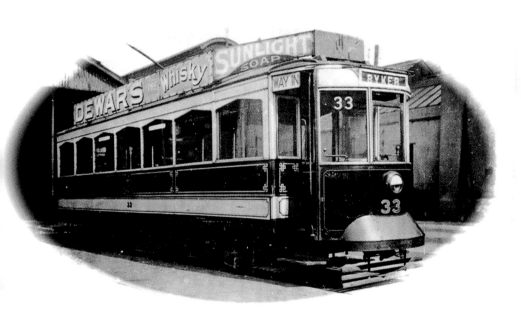

Some cities still have trams to get people to work.

Look at the horse in that field!

I like looking at horses. When my grandpa was a boy they used to do lots of the work that cars and lorries do today.

What sort of work did the horses do?

Milk was delivered to houses in a cart pulled by a horse. My grandpa said the sound of the horses' hooves on the road used to wake him up each morning.

Like an alarm clock!

Horses did lots of other things, too. Before there were taxis, horses were used to pull hansom cabs to take people where they wanted to go.

Wasn't it hard work for the horses?

They are very strong animals. One kind of horse is so strong that it was used on farms before there were tractors. It used to pull the plough and heavy farm wagons.

Does anyone know what that horse was called?

A shire horse!

How did people get to places that were a long way away then?

They went by train. Trains burned coal for fuel in those days, so there was lots of smoke and steam puffing out of the engine. They were very noisy, too.

Once my grandpa had a ride in the engine driver's cab. Imagine how exciting that was!

How did people in those days get to places across the sea?

They went in big ships. They worked by steam, too, like the trains. When my grandpa was a boy he went for a ride on a steamer.

There were still some sailing
ships when he was young, too.
They used the wind to carry
them along.

My grandpa had only seen one or two aeroplanes when he was your age. Aeroplanes had only just been invented.

26

They were very small and slow. There was no room for passengers either.

Yes, it's nice to get quickly
from place to place, but it
sounds like journeys were fun
in the old days, too.

Fun activities

This page shows lots of old forms of transport. Can you remember them all?

Make a chart like the one below to show how different forms of transport have changed over the years.

THEN	NOW
Horse-drawn milk cart	Electric milk float
Horse-drawn plough	
	Cruise ship

Imagine you could travel back in time.
Write about what it would be like to ride in one of the first cars. Imagine how excited you'd be as the starting handle was turned to start the engine. How would it feel to drive along the bumpy roads and be covered in dust? What would you do if it started to rain?

Interesting websites:
Find out more about the history of the motor car at:
http://turbo.discovery.com/amazing-cars/timeline/timeline.html

Lots of information about trains and railways:
http://www.familyandfriends-railcard.co.uk/cardholders/kidszone/railway-history

Discover why coal was so important to steam-powered forms of transport at:
http://www.bbc.co.uk/schools/primaryhistory/victorian_britain/children_in_coal_mines/

Index